Kick the World, Break Your Foot

Curated, Edited, and Explained
by
Asa S. Wagner and John D. Wagner

Kick the World, Break Your Foot

Published by The Conrad Press Ltd. in the United Kingdom 2022

Tel: +44(0)1227 472 874

www.theconradpress.com

info@theconradpress.com

ISBN 978-1-915494-22-1

Copyright © Asa S. Wagner, and John D. Wagner, 2022

All rights reserved.

Typesetting and Cover Design by: Charlotte Mouncey, www.bookstyle.co.uk

The Conrad Press logo was designed by Maria Priestley.

Printed and bound in Great Britain by Clays Ltd, Elcograf S.p.A.

Preface

We're a father and son team, Asa and John. After we'd collected, curated, and edited the aphorisms contained in *Kick the World, Break Your Foot*, we wanted passionately to write a knock-out introduction to prep you, our readers.

Working at our kitchen table – oh the seriousness of our mission! – we were certain we could convey rare insights into the instructively playful wisdom that our readers would soon find bursting from the book's pages. Other father-sons were out there maybe playing backyard ball games, but here our triumphant intellects were deducing multiple layers of meaning in ancient phrases, laying bare the timeless meanings contained therein. We often touched our own foreheads in revelation upon reading aloud the aphorisms container herein. One of us even uttered a genuine: *Whoa!*

And we quickly learned something in the editorial process: Many, perhaps *most*, of the aphorisms in this book are self-explanatory. In fact, we realized, that's what gives them their timelessness, and how their wisdom can be conveyed so fluidly across continents, and even across centuries.

At first, we thought we were powerless to add anything more to each saying. Any insight we tried to provide simply detracted from the aphorism's crisp, brave wisdom... But then we admitted that, well, maybe we could offer our readers a little help. Perhaps just add a glossary for those phrases that are so deep as to be potentially obscure? Take this one:

> Talk about tomorrow
> the rats
> will laugh

Or...

> He poisoned himself
> just to poison the tiger

Or...

> Even skilled hands
> can't hold water.

And so, we indeed added the glossary, which effectively doubled the length of the book! We kindly asked our publisher to separate the aphorisms from the explanation in the glossary, so that if you are reading along, and you 'get it,' there will be no reason to flip to the back of the book to learn what other layers of meaning we think you might have missed. The second reason we wanted the aphorisms and their explanations placed in different parts of the book is because we found that explaining aphorisms turned out to be sometimes like trying to explain a joke.[1] The explanation risked ruining the subtly, the delicateness, the light-brush-stroke quality of what the aphorism expressed. Take this one:

> Even honey
> tastes like medicine
> when it's medicine

Does it need a glossary to tell you what it means? Perhaps, but we suspect it will be immediately clear to most readers. Still, we didn't want to deprive our readers of any possible entry point into the fun wisdom collected here, so we 'glossed' each and every one of the aphorisms collected.

Are there any *Western* aphorisms? Well, anything we found that could qualify as a Western aphorism seems to be steeped in sulking and dime-store philosophy, *and* they are found mostly in song lyrics. At the 'high' end (ah hmmm) of the schmaltz scale, you've got the Grateful Dead (and full confession; John's seen *many* a Dead show, some he can even remember), you've got the phrases that end up on concert tee shirts, to wit: *'If you*

---

[1] We love the EB White quote about explaining humor: *Explaining a joke is like dissecting a frog. No one likes it, and the frog dies.*

plant ice, you're gonna harvest wind.' A seemingly insightful phrase, but after the band has packed and gone, ehhhh, maybe not so much. Or this one from The Eagles: *'You can check any time you like / but you can never leave.'* Or how about Pink Floyd (always with their dark nod to Orwell): *'You have to be trusted by the people that lie to you.'*

It's not quite wisdom, is it? Those phrases are more pronouncements in the *whoa dude* stoner genre; the kind of phrases that sound more important than they really are; they have no layers of meaning; they are all *surface*. A little better might be Bob Dylan: *'He not busy being born / is busy dying.'* Or *'there's no success like failure / and failure's no success at all.'*

But do these examples even stand up to a phrase like: *'Talk about tomorrow / the rats will laugh'*? Nope.

Hence our admiration only grows for the content we've gathered here for you. And so – no matter what Cardinal Point you hail from or what saints or sinners you worship – we will leave it at that, and trust you'll enjoy reading this book as much as we enjoyed curating the material.

Asa S. Wagner
Burlington VT, USA

John D. Wagner
Santa Fe, NM, USA

November 2022

Word origin

Aphorism (n): *From Middle French aphorisme, from Late Latin aphorismus, from Ancient Greek ἀφορισμός (aphorismós,* 'pithy phrase containing a general truth'), *from ἀφορίζω (aphorízō,* 'I define, mark off or determine'), *from ἀπό (apó,* 'off') *+ ὁρίζω (horízō,* 'I divide, bound'), *from ὅρος (hóros,* 'boundary').

Table of Contents

Preface	3
Chapter 1: On Optimism, Hope, and False Hope	9
Chapter 2: On People and Human Nature	19
Chapter 3: On Negotiation and Cooperation	37
Chapter 4: On Stupidity	45
Chapter 5: On Creation of Artifacts and Things	49
Chapter 6: On Futility and Exasperation	59
Chapter 7: On Acceptance	79
Chapter 8: On Being Poor	85
Chapter 9: On the Value of Discipline	91
Chapter 10: On the False Promise of First Impressions	101
Chapter 11: On Wisdom	105
Chapter 12: On Competition	113
Chapter 13: On Trying to be Something You're Not	125
Chapter 14: On Caution, Omens, and Sympathy	131
Chapter 15: On Leaders & Leadership	137
Chapter 16: On Patience	143
Chapter 17: On Making the Best of a Bad Situation	147
Chapter 18: On Accepting Consequences	151
Chapter 19: On Burdens, Luck & Fate	157
Glossary	165
Gloss: On Optimism, Hope, and False Hope	167
Gloss: On People and Human Nature	173
Gloss: On Negotiation and Cooperation	185

Gloss: On Stupidity	191
Gloss: On Creation of Artifacts and Things	195
Gloss: On Futility and Exasperation	201
Gloss: On Acceptance	215
Gloss: On Being Poor	219
Gloss: On the Value of Discipline	223
Gloss: On the False Promise of First Impressions	229
Gloss: On Wisdom	231
Gloss: On Competition	237
Gloss: On Trying to be Something You're not	245
Gloss: On Caution, Omens, and Sympathy	249
Gloss: On Leaders & Leadership	253
Gloss: On Patience	257
Gloss: On Making Best of a Bad Situation	261
Gloss: On Accepting Consequences	263
Gloss: On Burdens, Luck & Fate	267
About the authors	272

On Optimism, Hope, and False Hope

They shine with their own
sun and moon

If you know a song
sing it

Three feet above you
the spirits

They think their own
is the smart one

Sparrows that are a hundred year old
still dance
the sparrow dance

Even if the sky falls
there will be a little hole
to get out through

A little illness is a blessing

Be afraid only
of standing still

Yesterday should not use
too much of today

Distance tests the horse,
time the person

Adversity comes
learn from it
treat it as a favor

A tree is already a boat
but rice must be cooked

Times doesn't
come around again

Adversity yields flair

Aggrieved army
sure to win

Little sour fruits
ripe first
burst first

You try to sell the fur
when you've only just found
the paw-mark

Wants to cut bread
before the wheat's ripe

Heated water on for beans
before the plants are up

The feathers come first
then flight

Can't crawl
but he tries to jump

Iron hinge
straw door

Tomorrow's wind
blows
tomorrow

Never mind
what they say
go see

When he draws tigers
always comes out as dogs

Can't put out a fire
from a distance

In time
even the gambler
sells

On People and Human Nature

The rich
are never
as ugly

I wouldn't believe you
if you said they make bean cakes
out of beans

A thief who can't see
will steal even his own things

A blind horse
follows bells

If there is nothing you can do
pray

Better to die
of too much

Ask the mouth
and it will say
cake

Candy today
sweeter than honey
tomorrow

He cries
like a mouse when
the cat dies

I eat the cucumber
my way

She sees one thing
thinks she knows the rest

When someone is crooked
they see everything
and everyone that way

Even on dog turds
the dew falls

Dumb child
stealing a bell
covers his ears

He with ten vices
sneers at the man with one

Your own cold
is worse than somebody else's
pneumonia

Fish say
home water
doesn't look
like other water

Stingy,
he squeezes blood
out of fleas

Frog
soon forgets he
ever had a tail

He reads the menu
before he goes to the wake

What he can't help at three
he'll do when he's eighty

Even honey
tastes like medicine
when it's medicine

Finally gets
a horse, but then
he wants a groom

Everybody thinks
you had supper
at the other place

Sends the guest away
then starts cooking

The house address
means more than the kinship

Learns to steal
late in life
he will make up for lost time

Saved him from drowning
now he wants his luggage back

Has to drink the whole sea
to learn what it tastes like

To know
is to be sick

Doesn't know whether
they are riding
a stallion or a mare

Snow that falls on my hat
weighs lightly
when I think of it as my own

The world turns
through partings

Foot itches
he scratches the shoe

Can stand
pain even three years
if it's somebody else's

If word gets away
four fast horses
can't catch it

Rich?
even strangers visit
Poor?
even family members stay away

Full of danger
as an egg pyramid

Fate leads the willing

The traitor
has the best
patriot costume

Even a thief
needs an apprenticeship

Crooked branch
crooked shadow

Acorns arguing
which is tallest

Run out of wisdom
start boasting

No one has fewer
than seven
habits

The hissing starts
in the free seats

He borrows the flowers
for the shrine

If you want to blame
you'll blame

Says yes
when nobody asked

In every family
something's the matter

On Negotiation and Cooperation

Even with your aunt
You should bargain

Even the rich
prefer cash

Believe the cat
when even he swears off meat

Silver tongue
pays off
debt of gold

Day talk
birds listening
night talk
rats listening

You strike a better bargain
if you're not hungry

Talking to him is like
telling a fish about water

Touch it
as you would a bruise

If you get on
you have to stay on

The peddler won't tell you
that his melons are bitter

It's hard to dismount
from a tiger

Has one foot
in each boat

A melon on a house top
has just two choices

One be one side of the blade
One be the other
Together cut through metals

If you hand over the bow
you hand over the arrow

Most eyes will open
to look at money

Even heroism
can be bought

Always tell a man
that you'd thought him much younger;
that his clothes look expensive

On Stupidity

Wanted to know
where the sun went down
died looking

All he knows of the leopard
is one spot

Drank a shadow
thought it was a snake
got snake-swallowing sickness

Drops his sword in the river
to mark where the boat is

You need all your intelligence
when a fool asks you a question

The wise learn more from their enemies
than a fool does from his friends

On Creation of Artifacts and Things

Tree grows the way they want it to
that's the one they cut first

Three bushels of beads
don't make a string,
if they haven't got a string

Can't grow it
once you roast it

If it's too hot
there's no taste

A withered chestnut
hangs three seasons
while the good chestnut falls
after one

Cow in the stream
will eat from both banks

Easy
as riding
on a sleeping cow

No sleep
no dreams

No flower
stays
a flower

If the hammer is too light
it bounces

A knife can't whittle
its own handle

If something is too tall
part of it will be empty

Just dig
one well
that's deep enough

Beauty costs

Beauty
depends on the glasses

You can't sharpen something
once it's rotten

The rooster's cackle can't
call forth the dawn

When a thorn falls
there's a hole in the leaf
When a leaf falls
there's a hole in the leaf

Polishing won't make
everything a diamond

The pleasure is the flower
the pain is the seed

When something is too big or too thick
it can't be bright all through

One stroke of the saw
and the gourd is two ladles

Books don't empty words
words don't empty thoughts

Everywhere
birds make
a song

On Futility and Exasperation

Kick the world
break your foot

He burned his lips on broth
and now he blows
even on cold water

Without clothes
you can't even beg

He's all dressed up
but walking in the dark

A good tailor dies
with the end of a thread
in his mouth

You have to break the cook pot
just to cook the beans

Someone who eats
raisin cakes lying down
will get raisins in their eyes

You only need to have a toothache
when someone will give you something
to chew

A good story, sure,
but not ten times

It is like trying to smash a wall
with eggs

The dinner was more announcements
than dishes

They jumped into the fire
carrying kindling

If it leaks here
it will leak somewhere else

He's bald
yet wastes time
choosing hair ribbons

A plucked hair
won't go back into
its own hole

They come with the cure
only after he's buried

Even if you wrap up musk
twice over,
you can still smell it

To have no home
is like having a water bucket
at the bottom of a well, with no rope

A gentleman
would rather drown
than swim doggie paddle

Gets rid of one wart
ends up with two more

That person wailed all night
without even finding out
who had died

Gone like an egg in a river

She chased two hares
and now both have gotten away

When there are no hares left to hunt
he boils his hound

Invited nowhere
goes everywhere

She sees a horse
and suddenly needs to ride

You can pound bran all you please
but you'll never get rice that way

Eats all he wants
then upsets the dish

People, unlike sugar-cane,
are not always sweet

When I farm, the rain fails,
and when I steal, the dogs bark

Trying to put out a fire
brings on the wind

Even skillful hands
can't hold water

Can never reach
where it itches

One trouble goes
to make room for another

If you're stupid
life is harder

Just got it
in time to lose it

There's no honor
amongst thieves

Talk about tomorrow
the rats
will laugh

All house flies
eat with the best

Never mind,
it's across the river

Debt:
you have it
because you haven't got it

Reads a lot
yet doesn't understand

Save me from a small mind
when it's got nothing to do

That's all big thunder
but little rain

All bark
no bite

Burns his fingernails
to save candles

Truth is
what the rich say

Straightened too much
crooked as ever

Cows run with the wind
horses against it

Money: You're afraid you won't get it
then, you get it and you're afraid to lose it

Gone like today's flower
tomorrow

Ants on a millstone
whichever way they walk
they go around with it

One rat turd
ruins the rice

The flea bites
and the louse in punished

Just because you're cured
don't think you'll live

He poisoned himself
just to poison the tiger

On Acceptance

Close to death
you see how tender
the grass is

Life
is a candle flame
but a wind is coming

Even the bugs
are trying to run
from death

Every worm
goes
its own way

She loves even
the crow on her roof

Better than the holiday?
The day before

Got no clothes
can't lose your shirt

Good luck
bad luck
are twisted
into one rope

So close
to each other
they would hold water

Even a little impatience
can spoil a great plan

A bird does not sing
because it has an answer

On Being Poor

He's too stingy
to open his eyes

Old man's harvest
brought home in one hand

Desperation sends
the man to the noose
and the dog over the wall

Burnt tortoise
the pain
stays inside

When you're poor
nobody believes you

Wear rags
and the dogs will bite

Money drives out manners
poverty drives out reason

Poor man
drowned
nothing floated
but the purse

He is so poor, he knows
even his own pennies

He is so poor that
if he tried to sell anything
they'd think he'd stole it

On the Value of Discipline

Big pond
little ant hole
the whole bank falls in

Tap it first
if you've going to walk
across it

Smart
a cat rolling an egg

Somebody else
knocks down the nuts
but you pick them up

Listen
even to a baby

Coarse cloth
better than no cloth

Even do it sideways
if it gets you there

Quiet as
a crane watching
a hole over water

It's a long way
to the law
but my fist is right here

Flier
goes higher
than creeper
or leaper

Swallow
no bigger than that one
flies all the way south

He's the cripple
not his legs

So worked up
lucky he has two nostrils

One dog barks at nothing
thousands others
think it's something

She tries to catch the moon
as it floats by

If he flatters you
watch out for him

Do it hard enough
you'll do it

All those good deeds
some day you're bound
to get rich

Worm
gets at lion
from inside

If you get in a fight with a tiger
call your brother

Making money
is like digging
with a needle

When rich, time to dream,
but do not dream of riches
when poor

When luck comes
keep your head

On the False Promise of First Impressions

Pretty
but sour inside

Crow
has twelve notes
none of them music

Good tree
that's what the worms
thought too

That man has mastered twelve arts
yet can't cook his supper

The object of your desire is
most beautiful
just before

Warm it for ten days
cools off in one

On Wisdom

A liar
is an egg in mid-air

Old peasant sees statue
asks: How
did it grow?

So many have died with dark hair
So it's good to see it gray

Some steal when it rains
who don't when it snows

Can't have two points
on one needle

When you want to learn
what he's like
just make him rich

Prefer one who knows how
to three who don't

If you could see three days ahead
you'd be rich for thousands of years

When a rich man
turns poor
he'll start to teach

An eye can't see
its own lashes

Even from those we think are lovely
animals will run away

He lives one day
but what does he know
of the seasons?

Don't curse your wife
at bedtime

If the fish are going to be heartless
the water's heartless too

You owe more to the one
who brought you up
than to the one who bore you

Marry
your own size

You have to get out
of the game
to really see it

If you live somewhere long enough
it becomes
the center of the kingdom

Those things are as alike
as clouds and mud

On Competition

Adversary
is two people crossing
on the same log

Would try to eat broth
with a fork

He escapes from the deer
only to get caught by the tiger

Black dog
after a bath
is blacker

If you shut your eyes to protect them
they'll bite off your nose

Wait till he's falling
then push

If they're the same price
pick the prettiest

If you are a wren
with short legs
don't run after a stork

Silent
like the thief the dog bit

Where there's no tiger
the hares
swagger

Words
have no feet
but they get there

If the disease is unknown
the cure is unknown too

It's worse knowing nothing
than having nothing

If he comes from hell
you can't scare him with ashes

At first the hare
was in front

Caution
takes no castles

Hangs up a sheep's head
in his store,
but sells dog meat

A thief
plans even his naps

If a sardine threatens
who would know it?

Thirty-six plans
yet the best of them
is to fight

The ocean
doesn't fuss
about the streams

To the winners
the losers
were rebels

Nobody bothers
the bad boys

Smart hawk
covers his claws

Eggs
if they are wise
don't fight with stones

Enough mosquitoes
sound like thunder

If you can't smile
don't open a shop

Some squirrels jump higher than others
but sooner or later they
come down

The seventh month
sharpens
the mosquito's mouth

On Trying to be Something You're Not

He builds the Great Wall
in one night
asleep

He's a champion
shadow boxer

Needle thief
dreams
of spears

Thinks heaven
is a penny

He's so in love he thinks
even her acne scars
are dimples

He has a dress sword
But no pants, no belt

Laughs when
somebody else does it

He carries a harp
he can't play

They can't beat the big boys,
so they bully the little girls

Too scared
to be responsible

The crow
that tried to be cormorant
ended up drowned

The seed has hardly sprouted
yet you already know
it's sandalwood

You can whitewash a crow
but in won't last

It's only where pretty girls live
that he goes to look
for his lost hen

Scruples
can lead you
to hunger

On Caution, Omens, and Sympathy

Wade
as if it were deep

A widow
knows what another widow
is crying about

If the cock is silent
the hen will sing.
In a luckless sunrise
death is listening.

He keeps moving
because he doesn't know
this place
either

If you're going to be a dog
be rich man's dog

See what her
mother looks like

See what his
father looks like

What is coming
is uncertainty

Age comes by itself
but learning
does not

Anxious heart
flutters like a flag

Careful, he
ties his hat on

Secrets on earth
thunder in heaven

Even the gods lose
when they gamble

On Leaders & Leadership

Let's get there first
and *then* we can argue

Eat first
poetry later

The rats decide
the cat ought to be belled

A thread has to go
where the needle went

Water follows
a water leader

Ice comes from water
but can teach water
about cold

A judge decides for ten reasons
nine of which nobody knows

Before you beat a dog
find out who he belongs to

If two men feed a horse
it will stay thin

He is so kind
he treats people
as carefully
as a sore

Over a good person
a flame three feet high
stands guard

On Patience

If you ask
you're ashamed for a minute
but if don't ask don't know
you are ashamed forever

Asking questions
beats wit

Let your children
taste a little cold
and a little hunger

If you tell him
he won't believe you
so let him tell it himself

While folly parades
wisdom stands aside

Luck turns.
Wait.

Some places that were
mulberry fields
are now the sea

On Making the Best of a Bad Situation

If it's dirty work
borrow the tools

After winning
comes losing

Once I'm right
I'll fight anybody

If your house burns down
save the nails

A buried diamond
is still a diamond

When you're blind
you're not afraid
of seeing ghosts

On Accepting Consequences

If it goes alright
he'll take the credit,
but if it goes all wrong
he blames his ancestors

They steal the saint
while you're making the shrine

He's blind, falls down,
but blames the ditch

Cake on both hands
what next

Charcoal
writes everybody's name
black

He doesn't notice the hunger of others
but never misses when they are dirty

It's alright
you've nothing to give me
but don't break
my beggar's bowl

Repentance
never comes first

Coffin makers
pray
for a plague year

Bird shadow
crosses door
guests coming

Because they are family
you get to tell the guests
what to bring

Water
has no feet nor hands,
yet it can heal itself

The coffin
is a boat
and the corpse
a pilot asleep
sailing

You can't tell what God's
going to do next

Don't bother God
he won't bother you

On Burdens, Luck & Fate

Even when a tiny child
pokes you long enough
it starts to hurt

A hunchback
is always good to
his parents

It ate what I gave it
then bit me anyway!

Each a finger
can suffer

A blind fortune teller
can't see his own
death coming

If you do it wrong
you'll have to do it twice

If you must stop
do it under a big tree

Heaven
is a coarse net
but nothing gets through

Running away
he doesn't stop
at signposts

If it happened
it will happen
again

Some news wakes you
like cold water
poured into your ears

Every household
has its black pig

The sun gets in there
so seldom
the dogs bark at it

The rich
have relatives
for miles

As long as your pot's boiling
friends happen to be passing

Worth burning down the house
sometimes
for the fun
of killing the bedbugs

Hell has no door
everyone makes
his own

The more you want to own
the more you die

One sure thing about luck
it will change

GLOSSARY

Gloss: On Optimism, Hope, and False Hope

They shine with their own
sun and moon

This describes that friend of yours who has that inner light. They contain their own sun and moon. A gift, right, to be that luminous? These are the kind of people who leave you wondering where they get the energy to be that illuminated.

If you know a song
sing it

Is that show tune rattling around in your brain? That ear worm of a ditty dying to get out? Sing it.

Three feet above you
the spirits

Those who believe in a spiritual presence tend to believe it's not a distant influence but – like a guardian angel – right off your shoulder, ever watchful and protective. Nice comforting thought, eh?

They think their own
is the smart one

Every parent thinks their kid is a genius, facts be damned.

Sparrows that are a hundred year old
still dance
the sparrow dance

Ever go to a wedding and see that seemingly ancient uncle or aunt burst out with some outrageous moves? The dance inside them is ageless, like that of a bird that has no idea nor any care over when it will die.

Even if the sky falls
there will be a little hole
to get out through

Like many aphorisms, this is about hope. Even when there's a cataclysmic collapse, and the sky falls, it can't help but leave behind a hole that will provide your escape route. All hope is never really lost.

A little illness is a blessing

There's nothing like a common cold to give you an excuse to rest, without guilt, and withdraw from the obligations expected of your when you're at 100% strength.

Be afraid only
of standing still

Want to stay ahead of, well – you name it – love sickness, grief, loss, hopelessness, feelings of insignificance? Don't wallow in it. Step forward into a new day. Remember: *'The Wife of Lot got turned to salt / because she looked behind her.'*

Yesterday should not use
too much of today

'Don't look backward, that's not where you're going.'

Distance tests the horse,
time the person

This is a testimony to discipline and endurance. That's the measure of a person... not how far they have traveled.

Adversity comes
learn from it
treat it as a favor

As difficult as adversity seems when you're in the midst of it, be mindful that it happens to everyone. The 'favor' it bestows is the awareness that you're never alone when being challenged. You have not, despite your suspicions, being singled out.

A tree is already a boat
but rice must be cooked

You carve away the tree to *discover* the boat within, much as Michelangelo, the sculptor, claimed he 'released' the spirits in the marble. But rice must be fundamentally transformed, even transmuted, to become food.

Times doesn't
come around again

Seize the day, grab the opportunity. You never know when that opportunity will knock on your door, nor when you'll have time to answer.

Adversity yields flair

Adversity *reveals* who you are, and when you toss all to the wind in the face of it, some flair often emerges, some elan and panache.

Aggrieved army
sure to win

'It ain't the size of the person in the fight; it's the size of the fight in the person.'

Little sour fruits
ripe first
burst first

Those that rush to ripen are the first to rot.

> You try to sell the fur
> when you've only just found
> the paw-mark

Ah the age-old truism comes to mind: *Don't count your chickens before they hatch.*

> Wants to cut bread
> before the wheat's ripe

The person described here is simply over-eager to count the harvest, and the food it will produce. Patience and prudence are the lessons here.

> Heated water on for beans
> before the plants are up

The over-eager soul, getting ahead of themselves forgets that there's *'many a slip between cup and lip.'*

> The feathers come first
> then flight

As with flight (or success), you have to develop the tools that will lift you before you actually take flight. Be patiently realistic to soar.

> Can't crawl
> but he tries to jump

You've got to crawl before you walk, and walk before you run, and run before you jump. This reminds the authors of the Tibetan saying: You have to go slow slow to go fast fast.

> Iron hinge
> straw door

The mismatch is clear, so, make a door that matches the strength of its other components. But the deeper message here is telling: If you over-focus too much on one small aspect of a task, you risk depriving another potentially more important aspects of needed resources. Life is about balance, harmony.

> Tomorrow's wind
> blows
> tomorrow

Don't get ahead of yourself. A sailor would never count on today's winds if they were not departing until tomorrow.

> Never mind
> what they say
> go see

It always behooves one to form his or her own opinion rather than relying on the impressions of others.

> When he draws tigers
> always comes out as dogs

This is about how hard it is to break habits, plain and simple. It's only human nature to fall into patterns. Or are they ruts?

> Can't put out a fire
> from a distance

Often, you have to be there to solve a problem, rather than trying to direct others from afar.

> In time
> even the gambler
> sells

The gambler is always looking for a profitable exit, even the patient gambler. Question is, can you outlast him?

Gloss: On People and Human Nature

The rich
are never
as ugly

The rich, through adornment and with their ability to not really worry about the things most of us worry about (bills!), seem to always look prettier, don't they? It may be that worry and weariness take off the glow of what would otherwise exude forth as natural beauty.

I wouldn't believe you
if you said they make bean cakes
out of beans

Some people have lost so much credibility that others doubt even when they speak the truth.

A thief who can't see
will steal even his own things

Thievery is as much about insatiability for obtaining something for free as it is about the thief actually needing what he's purloined. This is true so much so that a thief will steal even his own belongings, if he or she didn't know the difference.

A blind horse
follows bells

If you are unable to find your own way, or even to see path ahead, you'll follow what is provided to lead you, in this case bells.

If there is nothing you can do
pray

When the chips are down, why not resign your fate to a higher power, even if you don't believe there is a higher power.

Better to die
of too much

An old saying holds true, even in the last moments of life: *I've been rich, and I've been poor, and I can assure you, rich is better.*

Ask the mouth
and it will say
cake

When human cravings emerge, uncontaminated by critical judgement, they say what they really want: *Cake!*

Candy today
sweeter than honey
tomorrow

Delayed gratification is *way* more interesting in theory than in practice. Most of us would take the candy now than wait another day for something, even if it promises to be a little sweeter.

He cries
like a mouse when
the cat dies

The mouse, despite its protestations and wailing, is very happy indeed that the cat has bit the dust. It's not hard to recognize false tears and pretend grief.

I eat the cucumber
my way

As a youngster, did you ever go to a friend's house, and look up to see the entire household staring in amazement at the way you ate your pancakes (rolled up tight and dipped in syrup, naturally). Other's mannerisms can seem odd to you, just as yours can seem very odd to them. *Do your own thing. You do you.*

> She sees one thing
> thinks she knows the rest

This is about that person whose overconfidence leads them to infer (often wrongly) that they can guess the whole from the smallest part.

> When someone is crooked
> they see everything
> and everyone that way

The crooked person (a cynic) believes that anyone who is not also a cynic is a naive fool. They can't imagine encountering people who don't doubt the intentions of others... when really, most of us give others the benefit of the doubt, until their actions force us to change our minds.

> Even on dog turds
> the dew falls

The beauty of nature, here in the form of dew, does not make judgement onto that which it adorns.

> Dumb child
> stealing a bell
> covers his ears

One of the authors, as a child, used to cover his eyes and say to his mother: *You can't see me*. Eventually we all grow up to realize it's not our perception that shakes the world, but the other way around.

> He with ten vices
> sneers at the man with one

Once you start *breaking bad*, and you don't fight the accumulation of vices, your misery seeks company. And you can't help but compete to be even worse, likely in the hopes of dragging down others with you.

> Your own cold
> is worse than somebody else's
> pneumonia

When you're miserable with sickness, even a mild one, it's happening to *you*, and you can't be convinced that others could possibly have it worse.

> Fish say
> home water
> doesn't look
> like other water

When you're out of your element, you know it. You feel a disquiet, due to strangeness, even though you'd probably be hard-pressed to say what's different about the 'water' you're swimming in, compared to the home 'water' you're used to.

> Stingy,
> he squeezes blood
> out of fleas

The conniving miser isn't so worried about how little blood they can get from a tiny flea. For the miser, it's the *getting* they live for, not the quantity of what they obtain.

> Frog
> soon forgets he
> ever had a tail

Why does the frog forget its tail? Because he sees other frogs just like him without one. He's happy to fit in and sees no utility in remembering when he was different.

> He reads the menu
> before he goes to the wake

Is the (pretend) grieving even worth it, if the meal the family serves up isn't up to snuff? The disingenuous plotter checks the menu first. A classic conniver!

What he can't help at three
he'll do when he's eighty

Habits stick with you. At first, they seem as light a paper Mache handcuffs, until they become so weighty that you can't move freely.

Even honey
tastes like medicine
when it's medicine

It's all about context and expectation, isn't it? Something 'sweet' doesn't taste as sweet when it's delivered as an elixir ...and not as dessert.

Finally gets
a horse, but then
he wants a groom

Some people are never satisfied and invent necessities that, for someone else, would be pure luxuries.

Everybody thinks
you had supper
at the other place

Some assumptions are convenient ones. A guest shows up for a quick visit, expecting to be politely offered dinner. But the host, maybe wise to the guest, assumes they've already eaten... even when that host, deep down, just doesn't want to break into the fridge.

Sends the guest away
then starts cooking

Who'd want to cook for a crowded room, when those house guest can just as well fend for themselves, at their own homes.

> The house address
> means more than the kinship

Ever show up to a glamourous party in an up-scale neighborhood? And instead of taking pictures of yourself and the hosts, you take pictures of you and your mates in front of the fancy pool? That's what this aphorism is about.

> Learns to steal
> late in life
> he will make up for lost time

When one surrenders to one's vices, a person can fall down the rabbit hole of not just allowing them to exist but to *feast* on them instead.

> Saved him from drowning
> now he wants his luggage back

There's the joke of an old woman on the beach whose grandson is swept out to sea by a rogue wave. She falls to her knees and begs God to please, *please* bring him back! Sure enough, a wave rolls toward shore, and it spits out the little boy, safe and sound. The old woman looks at the boy, and looks to heaven and says to God: 'He had a hat.'
Be thankful for what you get and not ungrateful for what you didn't.

> Has to drink the whole sea
> to learn what it tastes like

There are those who lack inductive reasoning, which goes from the specific to the general, and not the other way around!

> To know
> is to be sick

If you knew *all* the world's troubles, you'd be sick with grief and helplessness. Maybe ignorance is bliss, after all.

> Doesn't know whether
> they are riding
> a stallion or a mare

The dude or dudette described in this aphorism is just riding along, oblivious even to what kind of horse is in service. And probably happier for the not-knowing!

> Snow that falls on my hat
> weighs lightly
> when I think of it as my own

Remember the phrase: *He ain't heavy, he's my brother*? That's the lyrics to a Hollies' song, but it first appeared as early as 1924 (in *Kiwanis* magazine). If you were carrying someone other than a family member, you'd be constantly reminded of their weight, because you'd question whether it really is your duty to help. Ah, but when you *own* weighty things, weighty tasks, and think of them as yours, they seem to lighter. Snow on your own hat, when it's *yours*, is lighter than the snow loaded on you by someone else.

> The world turns
> through partings

Sad truth, no? Partings are loaded with the accumulated emotion of a relationship, whereas greetings, especially with new friends, have no such emotional heft, because you have not yet built the weighty bonds.

> Foot itches
> he scratches the shoe

When we first came across this aphorism, it struck us as mockery of someone dumb enough to scratch his shoe instead of taking it off and hitting the problem dead-on. Then we thought: Hmmm, maybe sometimes, it's not so bad to take a half-measure, to see if it gets the job done, before going whole-hog.

> Can stand
> pain even three years
> if it's somebody else's

Here we think of the lyrics to the American song by Steve Goodman: 'It's not hard to get along with someone else's troubles / just as long as fate is out there busting someone else's bubble, everything's gonna be all right.'

> If word gets away
> four fast horses
> can't catch it

Ever notice how quickly and efficiently people can communicate when the currency of the conversation is juicy gossip? It's impossible to stop. Even with four fast horses.

> Rich
> even strangers visit
> poor
> even family members stay away

The rich have eager friends everywhere, even when the rich don't want them.

> Full of danger
> as an egg pyramid

Oh do we ever step lightly around teetering piles, especially if they are piles of things as fragile as eggs. Something about to topple over is flat-out dangerous.

> Fate leads the willing

Often, the force of fate is as much an affirmation of where you think you should be headed, and not just a blind force pushing you along willy nilly. But this aphorism also implies the opposite: Fate will not lead the unwilling.

The traitor
has the best
patriot costume

Readers need to look no further than the disgraced ex-president, Donald J Trump, to see a man who wraps himself in patriotism when clearly he's interested only in power, himself, and not much more. Samuel Johnson, who no less than compiled the English dictionary, said it best: 'Patriotism is the last refuge of the scoundrel.'

Even a thief
needs an apprenticeship

Vices don't always come naturally to the wicked. Like any skill, they must be learned.

Crooked branch
crooked shadow

We think this one could well be understood as about *parenting*. If a child is the 'shadow' of their mommy and daddy, they will reflect their mommy and daddy's crookedness (if there is crookedness there) just as well as they would reflect their forthright stature.

Acorns arguing
which is tallest

It takes years to see how tall an oak will grow. Decades. So, it's simply fruitless for seeds to argue that they are tallest, when that can't be guessed and remains to be seen. Enough blather and bragging! Focus on spreading roots first.

Run out of wisdom
start boasting

Shifting the focus of a discussion or argument is usually done when the flailing speaker runs out of ideas or wit. What does he or she substitute? Wild claims of acumen in a totally unrelated topic of discourse. But people recognize when you run out of wisdom, and they are quick to see deflection at work.

No one has fewer
than seven
habits

Funny, there are also seven deadly sins. Coincidence? Luckily, the authors seven habits are all good ones, starting with brevity.

The hissing starts
in the free seats

If you ever have had the good fortune to fly first class on an airline, you'll notice that the most demanding passengers are the ones who just got the free upgrade. Some people who suddenly get something for free claim a companion right to criticize and be demanding... rather than just to be thankful.

He borrows the flowers
for the shrine

Think flowers left at a gravesite: When you borrow (as opposed to purchase) your contribution for a tribute, it screams cheap insincerity and disingenuousness. Come on, dig into your pocket, pony up, and stop being such a self-centered cheapskate.

If you want to blame
you'll blame

It's hard to change the mind of someone who's decided you're worthy of blame. That's probably because the blamer was already waiting for a reason to blame… and the perceived slight in question gave them just the excuse.

Says yes
when nobody asked

Obsequious people try to endear themselves by being agreeable, even when they don't agree.

In every family
something's the matter

Scratch the surface of the family that looks perfectly darling from the outside, and you'll see that they too have baggage. (Just hope the size of *your* family baggage is carry-on!) 'Everybody's got a sack of rocks,' as Elaine Stritch said.

Gloss: On Negotiation and Cooperation

Even with your aunt
You should bargain

The authors' immediate family numbers 26 people. Of all people, family members should not be given any quarter in negotiation for things of value, whether it's a clean towel during a Christmas visit, or the last bottle of wine in the fridge.

Even the rich
prefer cash

Cash is king in every culture. Anything else is merely a collection of promises and wisps of fragile paper.

Believe the cat
when even he swears off meat

Ravenous predators that are descendants of lions are never so hungry that they risk their health around day-old scraps. Trust the experts.

Silver tongue
pays off
debt of gold

Ever notice it's a 'silver-tongued devil' that can negotiate his own amnesty in sticky situations….Never the gold-tongued devil? (*Silver* was not always just a term to describe metal, but a word once used to describe soothing melodies and resonance, like the sound of a ringing silver bell.) But as the aphorism states, a silver-tongued devil can earn fortunes of gold with the right words, well-spoken.

> Day talk
> birds listening
> night talk
> rats listening

Elsewhere in this book, the authors have noted a curious fascination among aphorism originators for the clever savvy of rats, who – ever-conniving and utterly unsentimental – listen through the night for their opening. That's very unlike the eaves dropping of innocent day-time birds.

> You strike a better bargain
> if you're not hungry

Nothing concentrates the mind like hunger, when you'd likely bargain away your own sweet auntie for a bowl of soup if you've gone a few mealtimes without a morsel.

> Talking to him is like
> telling a fish about water

A fish does not *know* water because it had surrounded them since birth; fish lack the ability to comprehend the concept of water because they've never been out of it. Some folks are so daft they can't even conceive of the concepts you are using to express a truth so obvious that is surrounds them, yet has gone unrecognized.

> Touch it
> as you would a bruise

Some things need to be treated daintily.

> If you get on
> you have to stay on

Some events move so fast, you can't dismount or leap off for fear of deeper injury, even if you'd like to. In other words: *You climbed aboard. Now, go big or go home.*

The peddler won't tell you
that his melons are bitter

One of the authors used to work for a deli owner in New Jersey (USA) who would sell week-old pies to unsuspecting patrons after scraping off a 'protective layer' of mold. 'Are your pies fresh?' innocent shoppers would ask, to which the shopkeeper would say: 'Baked 'em this morning!' Anything to make a sale.

It's hard to dismount
from a tiger

Be careful whom you tie your fate to. Once you're riding atop a predator, roaring ahead in a full gallop, it's more dangerous to dismount than to take your chances surviving the wild ride.

Has one foot
in each boat

When one has a foot in each boat, it's easy to detect which one is sinking and which one will float. It enables one to pull a foot away from the doomed vessel, and say, as if you were wise all along: 'Ah, I picked the right boat after all. Knew it!'

A melon on a house top
has just two choices

Sometimes your choices are whittled down for you, whether you like it or not. You fall either to one side of the house or the other. There's no subtly nor shades of gray in an either/or scenario.

One be one side of the blade
One be the other
Together cut through metals

Simply put: Two heads are better than one. More poetically: stand back-to-back to fend off interlopers. Any combat vet would likely re-phrase this aphorism as 'Ok guys, let's circle-up facing out, and cover your sectors.'

If you hand over the bow
you hand over the arrow

You may think you've outwitted your opponents by handing them an unloaded gun, or a bow without an arrow. But now your potential enemy has the method (if not yet all the means) to turn against you. They are half way there.

Most eyes will open
to look at money

Those weary newlyweds at the end of the wedding, bleary-eyed, will perk up if you hand over an envelope on your way out, saying: 'Careful with that, it's stuffed with cash!'

Even heroism
can be bought

Even the most-honorable fighter who rallies to a cause is likely, at heart, a mercenary.

Always tell a man
that you'd thought him much younger;
that his clothes look expensive

Compliments and flattery will get you *everywhere*. Even Gorg the aging caveman probably blushed when Gorga grunted out: *Nice furs, you sexy young thang.*

Gloss: On Stupidity

> Wanted to know
> where the sun went down
> died looking

Don't underestimate the value of evidence that's right in front of you. And for god's sakes, take "yes" for an answer now and again.

> All he knows of the leopard
> is one spot

This describes someone who works at a glance, and thinks he knows the whole after seeing just a tiny part of something. This is an overconfidence in one's power of deduction.

> Drank a shadow
> thought it was a snake
> got snake-swallowing sickness

Here's the story of that person who leaps at the chance to be sick, and who is equally eager to invent the entirely new illness from which he or she suffers. You sit next him or her in the airplane, apologize for having a cold, only to hear them say they suddenly have a scratchy throat.

> Drops his sword in the river
> to mark where the boat is

This is right out of a Charlie Chaplin or Buster Keaton silent movie, where a hapless, helpless hero displays his comic stupidity.

> You need all your intelligence
> when a fool asks you a question

Some fool's questions are in search of something that is common knowledge to most of us. And that fool's questions are exhausting to answer, because you're providing remedial education in the process.

The wise learn more from their enemies than a fool does from his friends.

Enemies prevail by finding weaknesses, those soft spots you may not be aware you even had. But those revelations of your weaknesses can be instructive, if you are wise enough to welcome the lessons presented to you.

Gloss: On Creation of Artifacts and Things

Tree grows the way they want it to
that's the one they cut first

Behind this aphorism, maybe *deeply* behind it, is a sad lesson that non-conformists can sometimes be the first to suffer in a purge, if only because they have the courage to grow wild and stand out.

Three bushels of beads
don't make a string,
if they haven't got a string

Just because you partially possess the makings of some fine finished good doesn't mean you have the actual finished good in hand. Rough stones are not yet polished gems. Grapes are not yet wine. An oak tree not yet a table.

Can't grow it
once you roast it

Some things can't be undone, as when you turn corn seed kernels into popcorn, or garlic cloves into a spicey spread.

If it's too hot
there's no taste

It doesn't matter what food you're about to consume... if it's too hot, there's no subtly to its flavor. All you think about is how hot that damn dish is! But this aphorism reaches beyond food, doesn't it? Could it also be about lives that run too hot?

A withered chestnut
hangs three seasons
while the good chestnut falls
after one

Fruits that hang on so long, and try so hard not to give up, can entirely miss their purpose: their ripeness.

> Cow in the stream
> will eat from both banks

This one is just a brushstroke of a phrase, no? Nothing better than being about to 'play both sides to the middle,' even if you are a lowly cow fattening itself on grass.

> Easy
> as riding
> on a sleeping cow

There is ease to be had if your most-stressful trial is riding on a large docile warm-blooded motherly animal, who also happens to be asleep.

> No sleep
> no dreams

Rest is essential, even for the most eager, the most ambitious. It gives you the chance to imagine even greater heights.

> No flower
> stays
> a flower

No blossom is eternal; nothing blossoms continually. But this aphorism is also commentating on the passing nature of beauty, and of opportunity. Maybe it's even about love.

> If the hammer is too light
> it bounces

Match the tool to the task, always, even for something as simple as driving nails. (Also, see 'go big or go home' in the commentary, above.)

A knife can't whittle
its own handle

You may be able to perfect yourself on your own, but it's more likely the tool that's most effective is one that comes from without, not within. Can the 'blade' part of you effectively reach back around to perfect the 'handle' part of you?

If something is too tall
part of it will be empty

Match the vessel to the amount to be stored. Why waste space? The authors don't think there is a hidden lesson in this aphorism about life and love. It's probably the most literal statement in the entire book.

Just dig
one well
that's deep enough

The authors almost want to end this aphorism with '...damnit!' *and stop screwing around*. Half-measures and half-hearted attempts end up requiring double or triple the work, because what does not get done right the first time has to be done over again. And again. Do something thoroughly and right the first time.

Beauty costs

Looking beautiful costs time and money for the person seeking to look beautiful. But this cuts both ways. Beauty also garners high sums for those who seek simply to acquire it.

Beauty
depends on the glasses

How many time-worn cliches describe that beauty is in the eye of the beholder? This aphorism expresses with some levity, that sometimes, when something isn't perfect, you have to adjust your glasses... either to sharpen your vision, or to blur it.

You can't sharpen something once it's rotten

Only try to perfect something that is perfect-able. You can't do much perfecting when you start with something that's falling apart at the onset.

The rooster's cackle can't call forth the dawn

Time and fate work on their own time and at their own pace. They can't be hurried, least of all by a prideful rooster, cackling at dawn, who thinks he's in charge.

When a thorn falls there's a hole in the leaf When a leaf falls there's a hole in the leaf

When there's a hole in the leaf, or in your roof, or in your life, does it matter how sharp the implement was that created it? A hole's a hole once it's made.

Polishing won't make everything a diamond

As much as you may want to bring forth a gem through polishing it, you must have a rough gem to begin with. Desire and hopefulness alone can't always conjure forth gems, if there is not gem to be revealed.

The pleasure is the flower the pain is the seed

Think of the work – the digging, planting, weeding, watering – needed to produce even one flower. That's the pain part, the *seed work* that's needed to achieve the pleasure. Now think of this aphorism more broadly, where pleasure, the 'flower' of your efforts is an ambition realized. And the pain part is the long work you put in, which makes the achievement all the more satisfactory.

> When something is too big or too thick
> it can't be bright all through

A wafer-thin sheet of gold is gorgeous when backlit. A solid chunk, nah, not so much.

> One stroke of the saw
> and the gourd is two ladles

Maybe the solution to the problem is simply to cut it in half, where the halves suddenly provide two viable solutions (both of which you can drink wine from!).

> Books don't empty words
> words don't empty thoughts

Does the song exhaust itself when it is sung? Does a poem cease to be after it is spoken? Nope. Books and words are depthless, infinite resources that are not depleted with their use.

> Everywhere
> birds make
> a song

What's universal about birds? They sing and sound out. All of them. Everywhere. They are not silenced, even by war. A lesson there in finding *your* song no matter where you are?

Gloss: On Futility and Exasperation

Kick the world
break your foot

The authors selected this as a book title, because it needs very little explanation: If you kick a large unmovable object out of frustration, expecting it to react or bend to your will, all you're left with are broken toes, and an embarrassing tantrum. As with the all the other aphorisms in this book, a life lesson may hide beneath these six simple words: *Accept what can't be changed*.

He burned his lips on broth
and now he blows
even on cold water

Here's another phrase that explains this one: *Once bitten, twice shy*. And the authors add: Having erred, some people have a tendency to be over cautious, lest they make the same stupid, ridiculous, *how-could-I-have-been-so-stupid?* mistake, for the millionth time.

Without clothes
you can't even beg

You'd catch the eye, *maybe*, of Mother Theresa, if you expected a productive day on the streets begging while naked. Face it, you need to look *deserving*, even when you are penniless and asking just for a penny.

He's all dressed up
but walking in the dark

If you're going to *put on the dog*, and get all spiffed up, don't waste your adorning efforts by walking where you can't be seen.

A good tailor dies
with the end of a thread
in his mouth

Perfectionism is a *practice*, a way of being. The *doing* is the thing, up until your last breath. To die with the tools of your craft in, say, *mid-stitch*, ah, that's the mark of a passionate life.

> You have to break the cook pot
> just to cook the beans

If the beans are so hard to cook that they break the pot, they aren't worth the trouble. But is there a 'D.H.M.' here? (*Deep Hidden Meaning*.) Is anything worth the trouble of preparation, if it breaks the preparer, or irreparably damages his or her tools? Nope.

> Someone who eats
> raisin cakes lying down
> will get raisins in their eyes

If you're rushed and do things improperly (like eating almost upside down), something that should be sweet may turn quickly sour.

> You only need to have a toothache
> when someone will give you something
> to chew

The world has a way of finding your weaknesses, even when it is not looking for them.

> A good story, sure,
> but not ten times

We've heard that story already; shut up. Think dinner parties. Family gatherings. Church sermons. The folks at the corner bar telling war stories.

> It is like trying to smash a wall
> with eggs

Ensure you're using the right tool for the job. The *will* to do something (like, move a wall) won't alone suffice.

The dinner was more announcements
than dishes

Cut the pomp and blather, and for the love of Mike, serve up the promised meal! Dinners are for eating, not delaying a tasty bite listening to oration.

They jumped into the fire
carrying kindling

Late to the effort? Don't make it obvious by adding the kindling after the fire is already a'roar.

If it leaks here
it will leak somewhere else

One leak is usually a manifestation of a weak system and you can expect other leaks to follow.

He's bald
yet wastes time
choosing hair ribbons

Don't concern your pretty shaved head with things that don't matter to you, nor with attempts at adornment that would call even more attention to the very thing you're trying to hide.

A plucked hair
won't go back into
its own hole

Some opportunities are lost forever; moreover, regrets and panicked attempts to get a do-over might make things only worse.

They come with the cure
only after he's buried

Four cliches come to the minds of the authors: *Don't wait until the last minute. An ounce of prevention is worth a pound of cure. Too little too late. Oh, a'lotta good that does us now!*

> Even if you wrap up musk
> twice over,
> you can still smell it

Deal with the underlying causes rather than try to cover it up. (You could also try storing the musk in water, or heck, just throw it away.)

> To have no home
> is like having a water bucket
> at the bottom of a well, with no rope

Don't tell the publisher that we are padding the page count here, but even the authors are at a loss to fully explain this one. We just like the way it *sounds*, eh? Still, we keep coming back to two words when describing a bucket out of reach, and no rope to haul the water: hopelessly and frustration.

> A gentleman
> would rather drown
> than swim doggie paddle

Don't be too worried about your image or dignity when survival is at stake.

> gets rid of one wart
> ends up with two more

Better to live with a small problem than to try to get rid of it... at the risk of making it worse. *Leave well enough alone.*

> That person wailed all night
> without even finding out
> who had died

There should be no vanity in grieving, so don't be premature in expressing your emotions. At least find out who you're grieving for before your wailing starts. (Without doing so, you might risk mourning an undeserving corpse.)

Gone like an egg in a river

Some things leave before you can even come to terms with their passing, and they are swallowed up and forgotten with frightening ease.

She chased two hares
and now both have gotten away

Focus on assuring yourself of one meal, even if it's not as big a meal as you'd like. And here we can add the cliches: *A bird in hand is worth two in the bush*. This aphorism is clearly about more than capturing a rabbit. It's about being prudence when trying to capture opportunity, and – to pile on with another cliche – not biting off more than you can chew.

When there are no hares left to hunt
he boils his hound

Well, R.I.P. to the poor hound, first of all. T'was a nice doggie. But a hungry man hath little love for his faithful pooch when he himself is going hungry.

Invited nowhere
goes everywhere

This one goes out to that neighbor who just shows up at every gathering, invited or not... and all-too-often with a poorly tuned guitar, an over-loud voice, and an empty glass.

She sees a horse
and suddenly needs to ride

Can you say hyper-fixated ADHD? Sees cake, needs a slice. Sees a water fountain, suddenly thirsty. Sees a horse, suddenly need to be atop the saddle. And we'll add: *Monkey see, monkey do*.

You can pound bran all you please
but you'll never get rice that way

Ambition isn't always enough; determination and persistence can't always be transformational through force of will. And you *can't drink whiskey from a bottle of wine / can't get gold from a silver mine*, as Sir Elton told us long ago. (The authors are resistant to go to the gutter here, *but you can't polish a turd*.)

Eats all he wants
then upsets the dish

Oh, you licked the plate clean, but suddenly noticed the steak you already ate was under-cooked? Sorry, only the manager can comp the meal... and his shift happens to have just ended.

People, unlike sugar-cane,
are always sweet

People just aren't always nice. You might even find the Dali Lama kicking the wall in frustration if, say, they mix up his robes with another monk's at the dry cleaner and he's got to make a plane to the UN.

When I farm, the rain fails,
and when I steal, the dogs bark

Do good, and good will come. Do bad, and bad will come. *Instant karma* (good or bad) *gonna get you...*

Trying to put out a fire
brings on the wind

Remember at summer camp, when you tried to get away from the campfire smoke, and it seemed to follow you? Sometimes the very effort you make to solve a problem just makes it worse, even bringing on a force that seems determinedly spiteful.

Even skillful hands
can't hold water

Some tasks are beyond even a master's abilities, if the task (clutching and holding water) is an impossibility. But there's a larger life lesson herein, a parable. Have you ever tried to capture and hold something that was simply beyond being captured and held?

Can never reach
where it itches

This calls for (low) technology! Get a backscratcher, because pesky itches always seem just out of reach. But, as usual, the authors see a deeper meaning: That thing you desire seems always just out of reach, no? You don't remember the nearby itches you have scratched, because they are no longer bothering you. *You want what you cannot have.*

One trouble goes
to make room for another

For people who feel beleaguered by life, it seems almost as though they invite a new trouble to visit them just when they've dispatched the most-recent one. They are calamity magnets. We all know one or two in our lives. (And PS: the authors think beleaguerment is a choice, not an infliction.)

If you're stupid
life is harder.

Things happen to the daft because their stupidity deprives them of the ability to predict, prepare, and avoid... and if they can't avoid, to endure.

Just got it
in time to lose it

You won $50 in the lottery! Elated at your good fortune, you got home just in time see that you need a $50 fix on your car. Coincidence? The universe seems to know just how much money you have in your bank account.

There's no honor
amongst thieves.

This aphorism is as old as language itself, maybe one of the first cohesive human utterances. Why? Because even eons ago, when we were grunting in dark caves, chewing on super-rare Woolly Mammoth fillets, your neighbor Ork, having sunk to thievery and tasted its easy, ill-gotten gains, would never rise back to honor of his own accord.

Talk about tomorrow
the rats
will laugh

Fate makes itself known through its unsentimentality. In other words, each day the sun rises without distinction on all of us; fate does not honor what me and you had hoped for. Planning can be futile, as the rats have long known because they take what comes, knowing it can't be changed. Maybe they were the originators of the phrase: kick the world / break your foot.

All house flies
eat with the best

Prepare the finest feast, slave for hours doing do; set the table with finery and welcome your guests with fine wines. No matter how honorable your dinner party members, a common fly will swoop in and chomp down on the same meals that a king or queen might also be enjoying.

Never mind,
it's across the river

This describes our own concept of 'hassle tax.' If something is out of reach – and you have to cross rough waters to reach it – it maybe not be worth the trouble. Ignore things that are clearly unattainable. However, understand when something *is* worth it, and know how to convince yourself to attain it, where any obstacle can be overcome... *if you really want it.*

Debt:
you have it
because you haven't got it

First, not *all* debit is bad, if you use it to, say, obtain inventory that you sell for a profit. But all debt exists because you do not have something you wanted or needed. You owe something (debt) only because you are missing something else. *Trippy!*

Reads a lot
yet doesn't understand

There is a difference between seeing and observing. There are those who see (or read the movie script for) 'ET the Extra Terrestrial' and think it's about an alien that visits a cute boy. Those are the seers. Then there are the observers, who see ET as a *parable* based on the life of Christ: After descending from heaven, a love-filled alien stranger – mis-understood, shunned, and hunted down – attains a few faithful apostles. The alien stranger dies, comes back to life, and rises into heaven, promising to return.

Save me from a small mind
when it's got nothing to do

When a bright mind is idle, it tends to use boredom as inspiration for its next act of creativity, or at least industriousness. A small mind seeks mischief, often just for mischief's sake.

That's all big thunder
but little rain

Ever hear someone described as 'little engine, but big noise'? That's who this aphorism is describing. Someone who comes in all full of bluster, only to fail to deliver the goods.

All bark
no bite.

In some sections of the US, this is expressed as 'all hat, and no cattle.' In others, it's 'all hammer, no nail.' A NASA engineer might say: 'all booster, no payload.'

Burns his fingernails
to save candles

Keep your perspective on relative value. Are torched fingernails — where the pain last for days — really worth the price of replacing a cheap candle?

Truth is
what the rich say

Money talks. Often loudly. Often defining the truth, devoid of empirical justification.

Straightened too much
crooked as ever

Ever try to straighten a dented bike tire rim? It just gets worse and worse the more you try to fix it. As you set about your repairs, despite your best efforts, one dent becomes two, and a wobble gets wobbles. In a broader life sense, maybe you should just ride along with a little 'dent' in your personality, because the more you try to fix yourself, the more crooked you become... Leaving you to state another old cliche: *Leave well enough alone.*

Cows run with the wind
horses against it

Docile creatures follow the path of least resistance. Brave ones run head-long into it

Money: You're afraid you won't get it then, you get it and you're afraid to lose it

Funny thing, money. But think of it as a proxy for resources that you need to survive, because money *is* food, shelter, warmth. You have a natural instinct to secure them, and then, once secured, they are very worth defending.

Gone like today's flower tomorrow

When youth fades, it can't be retrieved. So, someone who regrets growing old might say: My youth is gone like today's flower, looked upon from the perspective of tomorrow. This aphorism is about the irretrievability of something that was once pretty.

Ants on a millstone whichever way they walk they go around with it

Ants on a circular millstone are minions subject to drudgery, no matter which was they turn. Their path is set, even if they change directions.

One rat turd ruins the rice

Famously, there is a true story about a surveillance camera that caught someone urinating in the reservoir of a small New England town. Even though the reservoir held millions of gallons, and the contribution of the, a'hum, offender was just a cup-full, no one in the town could apparently take a sip of water without bringing instantly to mind that... that... video. They drained the *entire* reservoir and started over. If you see a single rat turd in the rice, even if it's a batch of rice that's feeding a large party, it's hard to think there is not a turd, somehow, in every single bite.

The flea bites
and the louse in punished

When you get bit, your sense of indignation and revenge doesn't always rationalize who or what is really to blame. You go for the nearest possible suspect. Fleas fly off, while louse linger, and are likely to get punished for someone else's crimes.

Just because you're cured
don't think you'll live

We recently saw news of promising research that shows that doctors might just have drugs that can cure cancer! And we said: 'Oh good, now we can worry more about a heart attack.' Something's gonna get you.

He poisoned himself
just to poison the tiger

There's a fighter pilot's term called *target fixation*. You get so focused on the plane you are trying to shoot down that you'll sacrifice even your life because of that vengeful focus. Don't poison yourself by mistake when you really mean to poison just the enemy.

Gloss: On Acceptance

> Close to death
> you see how tender
> the grass is

Many people who are dying alas realize that doing small thing with great love and tenderness is what they should have been doing all along.

> Life
> is a candle flame
> but a wind is coming

We don't take this aphorism to be one of resignation or depression. Our very fragility is all the more reason to enjoy life while it lasts.

> Even the bugs
> are trying to run
> from death

Even barely sentient beings – dumb bugs – share a fear with the highest order of beings: A fear of dying.

> Every worm
> goes
> its own way

Here's an aphorism we can't fully explain, but it just rings true: Worms don't gather in tribes or packs. They are happy to wander, underground and in the dark. And isn't that a marvel?

> She loves even
> the crow on her roof

Some people appreciate everything, even ragged crows. And isn't that a lesson to everyone, in some small way?

Better than the holiday?
The day before

You gotta love this aphorism. You're about the go on vacation, and the excitement is palpable. The freedom of two weeks off work! The fun you will have! The meals you'll cook! Yet that may all be tempered the very next day, as you get stuck in traffic leaving town, and the kids start bickering over who forgot to charge the iPad.

Got no clothes
can't lose your shirt

As Kristoffer Kristofferson said in Me and Bobby McGee: 'Freedom's just another word for nothing left to lose'

Good luck
bad luck
are twisted
into one rope

You have to take the good with the bad. As we say elsewhere in this book: *One sure thing about luck. It will change.*

So close
to each other
they would hold water

Ah, that's love, right? Two people as one, water-tight in their affection.

Even a little impatience
can spoil a great plan

Plan your work, and then work your plan. Impatience is the hallmark of an over-eager player who invites mistakes.

A bird does not sing because it has an answer

To go full Zen on you, the follow-on thought here is: *A bird sings because it has a question.*

Gloss: On Being Poor

He's too stingy
to open his eyes

This is metaphorically about someone who won't open his eyes at the risk of realizing it might be better to see the world and share... than to close it out with selfishness.

Old man's harvest
brought home in one hand

The old man may have lost the power he had as a young farmer. But maybe the message here is that a meager harvest was all he ever needed all along.

Desperation sends
the man to the noose
and the dog over the wall

A dog that shuns its loyalty is a needy animal indeed. That same desperation for a human being can even inspire him or her to evil.

Burnt tortoise
the pain
stays inside

The authors are sure you've seen a bad scar and cringed at the pain you imagine was endured in the trauma. For a tortoise, withdrawn into its shell in a fire, the creature met its sad end privately. But can this shell be a metaphor for the 'shell' of, say, human loneliness?

When you're poor
nobody believes you

Economic powerlessness is often perceived as a lack of discipline, fortitude, or initiative. And that deficiency in the economic aspect of a poor person's life is often unfairly applied to, well, anything they say, even if it happens to be true.

Wear rags
and the dogs will bite

If you're trapped in misfortune and dressed in rags, it's hard to hide that in your face, your posture. Dogs can probably read that even better than your fellow human beings.

Money drives out manners
Poverty drives out reason

The rich have the luxury to be rude. They are easily forgiven... because the forgivers have ulterior motives. The poor can be driven to levels of irrationality out of pure desperation.

Poor man
drowned
nothing floated
but the purse

The purse floated because it was empty, containing no weighty coins. The man drowned and sank, perhaps heavy with worry.

He is so poor, he knows
even his own pennies

This fellow held on to his pennies so tightly, and stared at them for so long, that each one became a personal friend.

He is so poor that
if he tried to sell anything
they'd think he'd stole it

Distrust can abound and suspicions arise when you are poor and powerless. Show a dollar or a pound note, which you took out of precious savings, and people will wonder if you got it honestly.

Gloss: On the Value of Discipline

> Big pond
> little ant hole
> the whole bank falls in

Behind the little ant hole is a whole city, even a metropolis, with ant avenues, ant streets, and even ant burial grounds. Don't underestimate. Even ants.

> Tap it first
> if you've going to walk
> across it

It never hurts to be cautious. Never.

> Smart
> a cat rolling an egg

We too are occasionally impressed beyond measure by the cleverness of an animal now and then. YouTube has kept careful track of this on a global scale. Go ahead, google 'genius monkeys.'

> Somebody else
> knocks down the nuts
> but you pick them up

Nothing like avoiding the hard work of harvest, if you can just scoot along and grab what someone else has worked for, unfair as that is!

> Listen
> even to a baby

Youngsters, even ones that can't yet speak words, have something to say. You just have to learn their 'language.'

> Coarse cloth
> better than no cloth

Would you rather be cold with no shirt on, or warm with an itchy scratchy wool shirt? Sometimes, comfort is relative and a matter of perspective.

> Even do it sideways
> if it gets you there

Find a way to get the job done. 'By any means necessary.' Determination is often the mark of a successful person. Press on.

> Quiet as
> a crane watching
> a hole over water

Oh can't you just feel the silent patience of the watchful predator in this aphorism?

> It's a long way
> to the law
> but my fist is right here

This person is clearly at wit's end and taking matters into their own hands.

> Flier
> goes higher
> than creeper
> or leaper

This one explains itself. Be a flier, if you want to go higher.

> Swallow
> no bigger than that one
> flies all the way south

Tiny swallows, with determination, can fly around the globe. *It ain't the size of the person in the fight, it's the size of the fight in the person.*

> He's the cripple
> not his legs

Some people can overcome any obstacle. But this aphorism leans toward something larger: Are *all* deficiencies matters of perception?

So worked up
lucky he has two nostrils

The nostrils are venting this person's anger. And the observer is happy they have two of them, suggesting that if things got worse, maybe they'd need two more.

One dog barks at nothing
thousands others
think it's something

This aphorism is about something more grand than just dogs barking. It's about the misperception of authority. When one dog barks, others perceive it's for a reason, and worthy of being passed on without question. But the first dog may have been just sounding out for fun, or barking out of boredom, and not meaning to instigate a warning at all. Understand what you believe to be true, before 'barking' about it down the line.

She tries to catch the moon
as it floats by

The authors think this is an excellent concept for a children's book: The earnest child reaching out, thinking she is powerful enough to haul in the moon. A rather precious image, no?

If he flatters you
watch out for him

Elsewhere we have pointed out that flattery should be examined to detect ulterior motives. Not that you should be suspicious of everyone who says something nice, but there's no harm in being weary.

Do it hard enough
you'll do it

We love the Jimmy Cliff song, entitled: You Can Get it If you Really Want It. And the lyrics: *But you must try, try and try, try and try...* if there's a will there's a way.

> All those good deeds
> some day you're bound
> to get rich

We suspect this aphorism is meant to be delivered with humor. Good deeds don't make you rich but if you believe in karma, even instant karma, you'll do well to broadcast generosity and good will. The Beatles said it: *The love you take is equal to the love you make.*

> Worm
> gets at lion
> from inside

Patience and persistence will pay off, even when you're working against the odds, *if* you depend on your natural advantages.

> If you get in a fight with a tiger
> call your brother

Be prepared. Don't take a knife to a gun fight. Call for support. Accept help.

> Making money
> is like digging
> with a needle

It's *hard* to make money. And it sometimes feels as though you need to move mountains of dirt to do so, when the only tool you have is clearly not up to the job.

> When rich, time to dream,
> but do not dream of riches
> when poor

Dreams can distract you from the real work needed to attain your dreams. Work now, dream later.

When luck comes
keep your head

We again quote the Chinese truism: *One sure thing about luck; it will change.* So, don't let success go to your head, especially good fortune that isn't earned.

Gloss: On the False Promise of First Impressions

> Pretty
> but sour inside

Don't be fooled by surface beauty. 'Nough said.

> Crow
> has twelve notes
> none of them music

The ragged old crow can't catch a break, and that goes back eons. It must be the *way* they sound: plaintive, ragged, raspy, *suspicious!*

> Good tree
> that's what the worms
> thought too

If you see the merit of something and are poised to take advantage, rest assured someone else has seen it too.

> That man has mastered twelve arts
> yet can't cook his supper

Art as a way of life has to be accompanied by the ability to make a decent tuna salad sandwich. Full stop.

> The object of your desire is
> most beautiful
> just before

Just before *what*, exactly? Well, just before the defilement, the corruption, of a desirous, wanting gasp.

> Warm it for ten days
> cools off in one

On a micro level: How often have the authors spent an inordinately long time making a perfect cup of coffee only to have it cool down to un-drink-ability in $1/10^{th}$ that time! Was it worth it?

Gloss: On Wisdom

A liar
is an egg in mid-air

Any lie will eventually shatter when the truth comes out, which is always will. The egg in mid-air is full of messy potentiality, like a lie about to be exposed.

Old peasant sees statue
asks: How
did it grow?

This is the ancient Asian equivalent of a dumb blond joke. A peasant has no concept of how a statue is made, upon seeing their first one. Everything they know is grown, so why not this stone visage too?

So many have died with dark hair
that it's good to see it gray

For people who have lived through war or pandemics and seen legions of young people meet their sad end way too soon, imagine how satisfying it is to see someone who has lived a long fill life, and gone gray in the process.

Some steal when it rains
who don't when it snows

There's a reason thieves don't steal after it snows. They'd leave tracks, whereas the rain masks the path of the robber when the water quickly heals.

Can't have two points
on one needle

Another Zen thing we won't touch. Think it over. How useful is a needle with two points?

When you want to learn
what he's like
just make him rich

Wealth *reveals* a person, just as power reveals a person. A poor person can't be rude nor nasty, because they live on others generosity. Not the rich. Make a person rich and you'll soon see what they do with their (new-found) freedom.

Prefer one who knows how
to three who don't

We'll take the company of one wise person over a room full of dummies. We are sure you agree.

If you could see three days ahead
you'd be rich for thousands of years

All you need is 72 hours' notice of events that are about to happen, and boy oh boy could make some dough... and look darn smart in the process. Make yourself *half* that smart, get it *half* right, and you can be rich for 500 years!

When a rich man
turns poor
he'll start to teach

There's an American saying that goes like this:
Those who can, do.
Those who can't, teach
Those who can't teach, teach gym.

An eye can't see
its own lashes

If you are too close to something, you lose perspective. This may be especially true if you are trying to understand yourself.

> Even from those we think are lovely
> animals will run away

Animals fear cruelty, and having learned that lesson (we eat them, after all), they assume that even the most-beautiful of us are capable of it.

> He lives one day
> but what does he know
> of the seasons?

You can't really know the whole from a part, and this aphorism clearly urges a Buddha-like patience to take your time to get to know something.

> Don't curse your wife
> at bedtime

We'll leave this one alone, knowing that aggravated people aren't big on affection.

> If the fish are going to be heartless
> the water's heartless too

Ever been around a person who seems perpetually angry? The air around them seems angry too, like the heartless fish 'infecting' the water around them with heartlessness. The obverse is true, though. Loving people seem surrounded by loving air.

> You owe more to the one
> who brought you up
> than to the one who bore you

The work of child rearing merely starts with birthing. It's the hard work, and the daily demands of the day-to-day that defines a parent... not just who carried you for nine months.

> Marry
> your own size

When you see an enormously tall woman married to a diminutive fellow, you can't help but wonder how they make it work. The same with a couple who are mismatched not just in height but in girth. People of like size seem just naturally in harmony.

> You have to get out
> of the game
> to really see it

We have to go to a sports metaphor here. There are very few player-coaches for a reason. You need distance to get perspective. In sports and in life.

> If you live somewhere long enough
> it becomes
> the center of the kingdom

There is a comfort to staying in one place for decades, where your 'hound routes' are set and your domain is defined, as is your command over every part of it.

> Those things are as alike
> as clouds and mud

We love the expression that two things are 'as alike as chalk and cheese' – which means not at all. This aphorism is just another way of saying that.

Gloss: On Competition

> Adversary
> is two people crossing
> on the same log

You want some tension? Pit two enemies against each other on a narrow log.

> Would try to eat broth
> with a fork

This aphorism, truly explicated, would say: 'he's so clueless / he would try to eat broth / with a fork.' The authors suspect that we all know someone like that ...*and wish we didn't!*

> He escapes from the deer
> only to get caught by the tiger

You let down your guard when, *phew!*, you escaped from the attacking deer... only to leave yourself open to an attack from something much more vicious. There is a simple lesson herein: The survival of one attack does not lessen the possibility of a *follow-on* encounter with danger.

> Black dog
> after a bath
> is blacker

We just love this image, of a wet dog looking 'dirtier' (blacker) when it is wet. Nothing deep and philosophical here. Just a snapshot, an observation of irony.

> If you shut your eyes to protect them
> they'll bite off your nose

Put you guard up to *every* vulnerability. Otherwise, if you put your guard up just one place, you risk letting it down elsewhere.

Wait till he's falling
then push

Detect momentum, and help yourself out by piling on it. In a grander sense, if you detect someone else's weakness that you want to take advantage of, nothing wrong with giving it a nudge to, shall we say, *help it along*...

If they're the same price
pick the prettiest

When picking among equals in value, choose the item that most appeals to you in looks. Simple enough.

If you are a wren
with short legs
don't run after a stork

Recognize the capability of your competitor and appraise the chances of your success accordingly. Don't expect to prevail in a gun fight, if you brought only a knife to the duel. Don't challenge a long-legged sprinter to a race if all you have is short stubby legs.

Silent
like the thief the dog bit

The thief can't reveal himself in the middle of a robbery by crying out in pain when bit by a dog. He stifles it to keep from getting caught. Maybe you can think of when you've done this to not reveal yourself? Just sayin'...

Where there's no tiger
the hares
swagger

When the bullies are absent, the meek among us suddenly gain confidence.

Words
have no feet
but they get there

Words do travel fast. When the talk is juicy enough, words don't just walk or run... they fly.

If the disease is unknown
the cure is unknown too

The first step to curing a disease is to identify it. This is metaphorically true of anything that ails you.

It's worse knowing nothing
than having nothing

Let's say get a text from your bank that your account *might* have been hacked, and you *might* have lost all your savings. Would you rather sit there and not know your fate, even if it is a bad fate? Of course, you're going to immediately log-in to see what the damage is, because it's *worse knowing nothing / than having nothing*.

If he comes from hell
you can't scare him with ashes

You'll hear from combat veterans that nothing much scares them, given what they've seen. The same is true of devils who emerge from hell to the land of living. Not much scares them, given what they've seen on their home turf.

At first the hare
was in front

The tortoise-and-the-hare story is an enduring one not because the tortoise won, but because it did it with persistence and patience, while depending on the over confidence of its competitor. A timeless lesson.

Caution
takes no castles

Want to sack a castle? You might have to get out of your comfort zone and throw caution to the wind. The same is true when achieving any large life goal.

Hangs up a sheep's head
in his store,
but sells dog meat

Here's the nefarious merchant again, advertising lamb shanks, when selling dog instead. In modern life, we called this *bait and switch*. It's as old as time itself.

A thief
plans even his naps

Conniving people connive in every aspect of their lives, not just their thievery. Connivery is a *way of life*, not a single event.

If a sardine threatens
who would know it?

If a threat is to be taken seriously, you must look formidable. If you're too small to look formidable, increase your numbers.

Thirty-six plans
yet the best of them
is to fight

We all avoid conflict, and you can plan lots of ways to avoid it. But there can come a point where you admit that a confrontation is the only choice you have left.

The ocean
doesn't fuss
about the streams

Already satiated and well-fed, large oceans that are fed with many streams don't need to bother with any one of them.

To the winners
the losers
were rebels

Winners often believe they won because it was their destiny, their entitlement all along. Anyone who challenged that was merely trying to rebel against the natural order.

Nobody bothers
the bad boys

We signal how we want to be treated. Bullies, the 'bad boys,' exude a *don't even try it* air about them. And, you have to admit, this is pretty effective, and they are often left alone.

Smart hawk
covers his claws

Why announce your predatory capabilities until the moment you have to strike? It only gives your prey time to prepare.

Eggs
if they are wise
don't fight with stones

Choose your battles wisely, and don't enter one where you have a very low chance of success.

> Enough mosquitoes
> sound like thunder

There's power in numbers, even when just one in the number seems quite small.

> If you can't smile
> don't open a shop

Merchants that don't like customers are in for a tough life. Pick a profession that matches your demeanor.

> Some squirrels jump higher than others
> but sooner or later they
> come down

Time is the great equalizer, as is gravity; both are forces that eventually and inevitably do quite a good job of sorting out.

> The seventh month
> sharpens
> the mosquito's mouth

Mosquitos sense the end of the season and get more aggressive when they know, in July, it's *do or die* if they are going to breed and their offspring shall prevail. This is metaphorically true of anything or anyone who sense the curtain is about to fall.

Gloss: On Trying to be Something You're not

> He builds the Great Wall
> in one night
> asleep

Ah, dreams of grandeur, they are only dreams, and they do not confront the reality of the hard work needed to achieve something great.

> He's a champion
> shadow boxer

The person who only *imagines* prevailing in the boxing ring is a far cry from the person who prepares and actually does so. In your dreams, you are always the winner. In reality, ahhh, maybe not so much.

> Needle thief
> dreams
> of spears

When you have stolen needles, you aspire to spears. When you have stolen spears, you dream of guns. When you have stolen guns, you dream of cannons, etc. The grandeur you desire is often relative, invariably a level up from where you are today.

> Thinks heaven
> is a penny

If you have one penny and you get a second one, you have increased your wealth by 100%! Sometimes happiness is a matter of perspective, and doubling your wealth in one day makes it a good day indeed.

> He's so in love he thinks
> even her acne scars
> are dimples

Some of us can, through the blindness of love, see perfection where others see just flaws.

> He has a dress sword
> But no pants, no belt

You need a full complement of gear to go to battle. The sword is worthless if there is no belt, and no pants, with which to carry it. This is true of any tool you intend to bring to bear on any task.

> Laughs when
> somebody else does it

Go along to get along sometimes makes people laugh, even when they don't find something funny.

> He carries a harp
> he can't play

Maybe this could be re-written as: *he carries a book he can't read*, or a *song sheet he can't sing*. Is this person adorning himself to admired for a skill that he doesn't really have?

> They can't beat the big boys,
> so they bully the little girls

Universally, bullies will take out their grievances on the powerless, and they will keep searching down the chain of victims until they find one weaker than they.

> Too scared
> to be responsible

Here's a description of a coward who simply won't own up to something, out of fear that they will get their just desserts.

> The crow
> that tried to be cormorant
> ended up drowned

Don't try to something you are not.

> The seed has hardly sprouted
> yet you already know
> it's sandalwood

Many sprouts, and indeed it's true of some people, show evidence of what or who they will become, even when they very first emerge into the world.

> You can whitewash a crow
> but in won't last

It's hard to mask in the long term who or what you are. But that doesn't stop people from trying.

> It's only where pretty girls live
> that he goes to look
> for his lost hen

We know this guy, cleverly seeking an excuse to make time with the girls who have caught his eye.

> Scruples
> can lead you
> to hunger

Someone who is honest to a fault can be so honest as to defeat their own intentions, especially if they are playing against people who have no qualms about going to the 'dark side' to get what they want.

Gloss: On Caution, Omens, and Sympathy

> Wade
> as if it were deep

Be cautious. Test the waters before plunging in. This is true when crossing a literal river... or a figurative one.

> A widow
> knows what another widow
> is crying about

Often you have to experience something to truly know what others have experienced. Some grief can't be imagined.

> If the cock is silent
> the hen will sing.
> In a luckless sunrise
> death is listening

Wow, that's dark! There's a mixed sense of both fate and foreboding. We are at a loss to explain it, and – like some other aphorisms in this book – just rest in the Zen of the resonant image.

> He keeps moving
> because he doesn't know
> this place
> either

One can recognize a 'home' even when one has never been there before.

> If you're going to be a dog
> be rich man's dog

Among various fates, if you must be a supplicant, be a supplicant to a kind master, with resources.

> See what her
> mother looks like
> See what his
> father looks like

Want to see how someone will age? Don't look at him or her when they are 21, all glorious in youthful splendor. Look at their mom or their dad; they are the older versions.

> What is coming
> is uncertainty

Life is as fragile as it is unpredictable. They only thing certain is uncertainty.

> Age comes by itself
> but learning
> does not

You can't stop the momentum of age. But the momentum of learning must be invited; it takes work. Age is effortless.

> Anxious heart
> flutters like a flag

We love this image of a frantic flag in the wind. It's perfect for describing anxiousness.

> Careful, he
> ties his hat on

Prepare well, tie on that hat, long before the wind blows.

> Secrets on earth
> thunder in heaven

If heaven is populated by angels and gods who see all, there are no secrets. Indeed, secrets are louder for what, on earth, they work to suppress.

Even the gods lose when they gamble

We are all subject to chance, whether we are humble earthlings, or heavenly creatures. There's no escaping it.

Gloss: On Leaders & Leadership

Let's get there first
and *then* we can argue

Two travelers disagree on the road to take. Both are right, because both roads will get them there. But, honestly, let's commit to one path, get on our way, and *then* argue over whether one way would have been faster than the other.

Eat first
poetry later

Art is lovely, with poetry the highest form. But you have to take care of the necessities of life before you thrive as a creative being. A starving artist will think of food for a long time before coming up with a great opening line to his or her opus.

The rats decide
the cat ought to be belled

Well of course the rat is looking for an unfair advantage here, a head start in getting away. The cat, who never wants to be detected, would never elect to put a bell on itself.

A thread has to go
where the needle went

Some fates just pull you along, and you have no choice but to follow.

Water follows
a water leader

We will say it again: Some fates just pull you along, and you have no choice but to follow.

> Ice comes from water
> but can teach water
> about cold

This is one of those Zen koan-like aphorisms that you just have to stare at and think over. Understanding it may not be the point.

> A judge decides for ten reasons
> nine of which nobody knows

Asked to explain a verdict, a judge may say one of the reasons for a decision. But isn't that just to avoid saying that their gut was what they really trusted?

> Before you beat a dog
> find out who he belongs to

Oh sure, dogs are easily victims for cruel people to take out their frustrations... until they realize they've whipped the cherished dog of the minister of the police. And *now* guess who will take a beating?

> If two men feed a horse
> it will stay thin

One man will assume the other is adequately feeding the horse, and be frugal due to that assumption. The second man thinks the same. The horse suffers in the balance.

> He is so kind
> he treats people
> as carefully
> as a sore

Be kind and gentle, always.

> Over a good person
> a flame three feet high
> stands guard

We've met those people now and then who are so kind and loving, they seem protected. And deservedly so.

Gloss: On Patience

> If you ask
> you're ashamed for a minute
> but if don't ask don't know
> you are ashamed forever

The only stupid question is one that is unasked.

> Asking questions
> beats wit

Wit, and laughing off a challenge, are great deflectors. But why not *ask*, and know... so you don't feel the need to change the subject?

> Let your children
> taste a little cold
> and a little hunger

If parents make it too easy on a child, he or she will not be tested by adversity. Adversity will, in the end, make them stronger not weaker.

> If you tell him
> he won't believe you
> so let him tell it himself

Some people are so suspicious, they believe only themselves, and can't be told, even by genuine truth sayers.

> While folly parades
> wisdom stands aside

Wisdom is patient, even letting pomp prevail – *go ahead, have your fun!* – while wisdom lies in wait for the folly to subside, as it always eventually does.

> Luck turns
> Wait

Again: *One sure thing about luck / it will change.* Patience.

Some places that were mulberry fields are now the sea

The sea is patient and persistent, and maybe it's a lesson for living life. Conversely, the mulberry fields stand for the impermanence of things we once thought rooted in solid ground.

Gloss: On Making Best of a Bad Situation

If it's dirty work
borrow the tools

It's unfair, and something the authors would never really do, but why sully your own tools when you know the work will be messy?

After winning
comes losing

There is a ying/yang to life. First comes pleasure, then comes pain. First comes a lucky streak, then a losing one.

Once I'm right
I'll fight anybody

Again: *It ain't the size of the person in the fight, it's the size of the fight in the person.* When you're right and know it, there's a fierceness within!

If your house burns down
save the nails

Got nothing but a house in ashes? Start over, painful as it is, because the ashes may contain the very tools needed to rebuild.

A buried diamond
is still a diamond

A buried treasure is still a treasure. It just needs to be discovered, and dusted off.

When you're blind
you're not afraid
of seeing ghosts

You can't scare me, because I can't even see what I'm supposed to be afraid of! Maybe there's a benefit to being blind to the things that scare others.

Gloss: On Accepting Consequences

> If it goes alright
> he'll take the credit,
> but if it goes all wrong
> he blames his ancestors

Oh the globe-spanning persistence of excuse making! To the excuse maker, it's always someone else's fault when things go belly up... but credit will be wholly and readily taken by that same person, even when they don't deserve it.

> They steal the saint
> while you're making the shrine

One can get so distracted by adornment and shrine-making that they lose sight of the reason they are worshipping something in the first place.

> He's blind, falls down,
> but blames the ditch

It's always someone else's fault, for some people, isn't it?

> Cake on both hands
> what next

There's nothing wrong with enduring the minor indignity of licking one's fingers, when both hands are covered with sticky cake.

> Charcoal
> writes everybody's name
> black

There are great equalizers in life. One of them is that your name, along with the names of a president or prime minister, all look very much the same when written in black ink. Comforting in a way, no?

> He doesn't notice the hunger of others
> but never misses when they are dirty

A cruel, unjust fact is that even the homeless are expected by some well-fed passersby to look *deserving*, to have taken the trouble to clean up before it's deemed they are worthy of a meal.

> It's alright
> you've nothing to give me
> but don't break
> my beggar's bowl

It's hard to explain the cruelty of someone who would break the bowl of a beggar, but it's likely out of indignation that they are being asked to freely give up something they have worked hard to *earn*.

> Repentance
> never comes first

Would the perpetrator feel as guilty, bowing down in repentance, if they had not been caught? Probably not. That's why repentance *never comes first*...

> Coffin makers
> pray
> for a plague year

One thing about the funeral business: It gets better all the time! An unsentimental funeral director may not exactly mind a plague year. Did the covid test makers mind selling box after box of test kits as the pandemic ripped across the globe?

> Bird shadow
> crosses door
> guests coming

Ah the approaching guests have spooked the birds! But there's some foreboding here, isn't there, in the shadows? Maybe all guests are not always welcome?

> Because they are family
> you get to tell the guests
> what to bring

Nothing like bossing your brother or sister around when you're writing the menu for a big party. After all, it's your house, and you're stuck cleaning it afterwards... so why shouldn't you ask your big sis to make her famous fruit salad?

> Water
> has no feet nor hands,
> yet it can heal itself

Another Zen image. Just read it and contemplate, imagining a choppy body of water that settles out to a calm mirrored surface.

> The coffin
> is a boat
> and the corpse
> a pilot asleep
> sailing

In this image, the dead, resting in their coffins, seem to be piloting their next voyage. Comforting in a way.

> You can't tell what God's
> going to do next

Three recurring and resonant themes in many of these aphorisms are: the uncertainty of life, the unpredictability of fate, and that fact that we are subject to the whims of God.

> Don't bother God
> he won't bother you

Be good, and you'll be invisible to a wrathful God. (Yeah, good luck with that!)

Gloss: On Burdens, Luck & Fate

> Even when a tiny child
> pokes you long enough
> it starts to hurt

Little things that seem harmless, done over and over, can eventually accumulate, and amass to create genuine troubles.

> A hunchback
> is always good to
> his parents

A friend in need is a friend indeed.

> It ate what I gave it
> then bit me anyway!

There's an a genuine (and well-deserved!) indignation when something bites the hand that feeds it. Like WTF dude?

> Each a finger
> can suffer

Suffering can be suffering even when it's not the whole body that's injured. Even the smallest part of us can suffer, and sometimes greatly.

> A blind fortune teller
> can't see his own
> death coming

Spooky! But the blindness here is blindness at-large, *metaphorical* blindness. We are often blind to the fates we ourselves are subject to, even when we clearly see their effects in others.

> If you do it wrong
> you'll have to do it twice

There always seems to be time to re-do something you felt you had to complete in a hurry, having botched it up as a result of your impatience.

> If you must stop
> do it under a big tree

If you have a choice, pick the path of ease. As the Spanish say: *Walk on the shady side*.

> Heaven
> is a coarse net
> but nothing gets through

This is another way of saying that the wheels of fate grind very slowly, but, over time, they grind very finely, catching all.

> Running away
> he doesn't stop
> at signposts

Frantic to get away, and feeling justified in your flight, why start obeying someone else's rules? Rebels run heedless.

> If it happened
> it will happen
> again

Just because something happens once doesn't preclude it from happening again, as if you can say, *phew, glad we are done with that!*

> Some news wakes you
> like cold water
> poured into your ears

There's bad news in all of our futures. It's just life. And sometimes it will come as a rude and unwelcome surprise.

Every household
has its black pig

There's always that sister, that brother, that cousin, that uncle or aunt, isn't there? That one that stands out so clearly from the herd, and not always for the best of reasons.

The sun gets in there
so seldom
the dogs bark at it

The dog is surprised, even by its good fortune of being bathed in the sun, when it normally lives in the shadows.

The rich
have relatives
for miles

When you are a person of good fortune and wealth, every relative will eventually find you, and, you know, reach out, just staying in touch; just saying hi... adding: *And you remember that our mothers were sisters, right?*

As long as your pot's boiling
friends happen to be passing

Nothing draws in needy friends for a quick visit more than a full pot of soup.

Worth burning down the house
sometimes
for the fun
of killing the bedbugs

Oh the irrationality that revenge can inspire! You want your pound of flesh, even if it means killing the object of your grievance... *and yourself* in the process!

> Hell has no door
> everyone makes
> his own

You create your own fate, even to the point of building (through your actions) the very door through which you step into misery, should you choose that.

> The more you want to own
> the more you die

Attachment to things, desire, that's what the Buddha said will lead to suffering, and that's what this aphorism addresses.

> One sure thing about luck
> it will change

The authors have cited this quote numerous times in the book, because it is our favorite and needs no explanation. We have indeed saved the best one for last.

The editors especially wish to thank and acknowledge the pioneering work of W.S. Merwin, whose work on Asian sayings, published nearly fifty years ago, in part inspired this collection.

-ends-

ASA S. WAGNER is a writer and photographer living in Burlington VT, USA. He recently wrote and directed *The British Play*, which was produced on stage in San Francisco at California College of the Arts. He is nearing completion on his forthcoming novel, *A Potentially Hazardous Affair*, even as other book projects teem in his head. *Kick the World / Break Your Foot* is his first book.

JOHN D. WAGNER is a poet, young-adult novelist, non-fiction writer, and photographer who lives in Santa Fe, NM, USA. He works for a boutique investment bank, matching buyers and sellers of businesses, and he frequently writes articles and books on mergers and acquisitions topics. *Kick the World / Break Your Foot* is his 24th book.

INSTAGRAM: Kick_the_World_Break_Your_Foot

COVER ART: by Joe Mullins.